MY MASTER

MY MASTER

WITH AN APPENDED EXTRACT

FROM THE

THEISTIC QUARTERLY REVIEW

SWAMI VIVEKANANDA

GYAN

Published by

Gyan Publishing House
5, Ansari Road
Daryaganj, New Delhi-110002
Phone: 011-47034999, 9811692060
E-mail: books@gyanbooks.com

Distribution Network
gyanbooks.com
India, USA, Canada, UK, Australia

ISBN: 978-93-6780-385-1 (PB)

First Published, 1901

2nd Impression 2024

Printed at: Gyan Press, Delhi.

MY MASTER
Author: SWAMI VIVEKANANDA

MY MASTER

MY MASTER

BY THE

SWÂMI VIVEKÂNANDA

WITH AN APPENDED EXTRACT

FROM THE

THEISTIC QUARTERLY REVIEW

Om Namo Bhagavate Râmakrishnâya!

(Salutation to Blessed Râmakrishna!)

PREFACE

THE following lecture, which was delivered in New York under the auspices of the Vedânta Society, describes briefly one of the most remarkable men that India has given to the nineteenth century. He was known as PARAMHAMSA SRIMAT RAMAKRISHNA, and is regarded by thousands of his fellow-countrymen as a Divine Incarnation, although he would not claim for himself any high position. The influence of his teachings is making itself felt in all parts of India, and has even extended to Europe and America.

The frontispiece represents the temple near which he passed the last years of his life. He lived in a small house in the extensive gardens surrounding the temple, and great crowds of people came to listen to his words. Since his death a yearly festival has been held on the anniversary of his birth, and is each year attended by increasing numbers. The title *Paramhamsa* means, literally, "Great Soul," and is given by the Hindus to such men only as have attained to the highest spiritual illumination. *Srimat* is a title of respect, and is used here in the sense of "most revered."

THE EDITOR.

MY MASTER

"WHENEVER virtue subsides and vice prevails, I come down to help mankind," declares Krishna, in the Bhagavad Gitâ. Whenever this world of ours, on account of growth, on account of added circumstances, requires a new adjustment, a wave of power comes, and as man is acting on two planes, the spiritual and the material, waves of adjustment come on both planes. On the one side, of adjustment on the material plane, Europe has mainly been the basis during modern times, and of the adjustment on the other, the spiritual plane, Asia has been the basis throughout the history of the world. To-day, man requires one more adjustment on the spiritual plane; to-day, when material ideas are at the height of their glory and power; to-day, when man is likely to forget his divine nature, through his growing dependence on matter, and is likely to be reduced to a mere money-making machine, an adjustment is necessary, and the power is coming, the voice has spoken, to drive away the clouds of gathering materialism. The power has been set in motion which, at no distant date, will bring unto mankind once more the memory of their real nature, and again the place from which this power will start will be Asia. This world of ours is on the plan of the division of labor. It is vain to say that one man shall possess everything. Yet how childish we are! The baby in his childishness thinks that his doll is the only possession that is to be coveted in this whole universe. So a nation which is great in the possession of material powers thinks that that is all that is to be coveted, that that is all that is meant by progress, that that is all that is meant by civilization, and if there are other nations which do not care to possess, and do not possess these powers, they are not fit to live, their whole existence is useless. On the other hand, another nation may think that mere material civilization is utterly useless. From the Orient came the voice which once told the world that if a man possess everything that is under the sun or above it, and does not possess spirituality, what matters it? This is the Oriental type, the other is the Occidental type.

Each of these types has its grandeur, each has its glory. The present adjustment will be the harmonizing, the mingling of these two ideals. To the Oriental, the world of spirit is as real as to the Occidental is the world of senses. In the spiritual, the Oriental finds everything he wants or hopes for; in it he finds all that makes life real to him. To the Occidental he is a dreamer; to the Oriental, the Occidental is a dreamer, playing with dolls of five minutes, and he laughs to think that grown-up men and women should make so much of a handful of matter which they will have to leave sooner or later. Each calls the other a dreamer. But the Oriental ideal is as necessary for the progress of the human race as is the Occidental, and I think it is more necessary. Machines never made mankind happy, and never will make. He who is trying to make us believe this, will claim that happiness is in the machine, but it is always in the mind. It is the man who is lord of his mind who alone can become happy, and none else. But what, after all, is this power of machinery? Why should a man who can send a current of electricity through a wire be called a very great man, and a very intelligent man? Does not nature do a million times more than that every moment? Why not then fall down and worship nature? What matters it if you have power over the whole of the world, if you have mastered every atom in the universe? That will not make you happy unless you have the power of happiness in yourself, until you have conquered yourself. Man is born to conquer nature, it is true, but the Occidental means by "nature" only the physical or external nature. It is true that external nature is majestic, with its mountains, and oceans, and rivers, and with its infinite powers and varieties. Yet there is a more majestic internal nature of man, higher than the sun, moon and stars, higher than this earth of ours, higher than the physical universe, transcending these little lives of ours; and it affords another field of study. There the Orientals excel, just as the Occidentals excel in the other. Therefore it is fitting that, whenever there is a spiritual adjustment, it should come from the Orient. It is also fitting that when the Oriental wants to learn about machine-making he should sit at the feet of the Occidental and learn from him. When the Occident wants to learn about the spirit, about God, about the soul, about the meaning and the mystery of this universe, she must sit at the feet of the Orient to learn.

I am going to present before you the life of one man who has been the mover of such a wave in India. But before going into the life of this man I will try to present before you the secret of India, what India means. If those whose eyes have been blinded by the glamor of material things, whose whole dedication of life is to eating and drinking and enjoying, whose whole ideal of possession is lands and gold, whose whole ideal of pleasure is in the sensations, whose god is money, and whose goal is a life of ease and comfort in this world, and death after that, whose minds never look forward, and who rarely think of anything higher than the sense objects in the midst of which they live, if such as these go to India, what do they see? Poverty, squalor, superstition, darkness, hideousness everywhere. Why? Because in their minds enlightenment means dress, education, social politeness. Whereas Occidental nations have used every effort to improve their material position, India has done differently. There lives the only race in the world which, in the whole history of humanity, never went beyond their frontiers to conquer anyone, who never coveted that which belonged to anyone else, and whose only fault was that their lands were so fertile, and their wits so keen, that they accumulated wealth by the hard labor of their hands, and so tempted other nations to come and despoil them. They are contented to be despoiled, and to be called barbarians, and in return they want to send to this world visions of the Supreme, to lay bare for the world the secrets of human nature, to rend the veil that conceals the real man, because they know the dream, because they know that behind this materialism lives the real divine nature of man which no sin can tarnish, no crime can spoil, no lust can kill, which the fire cannot burn, nor the water wet, which heat cannot dry, nor death kill; and to them this true nature of man is as real as is any material object to the senses of an Occidental. Just as you are brave to jump at the mouth of a cannon with a hurrah; just as you are brave in the name of patriotism to stand up and give up your lives for your country, so are they brave in the name of God. There it is that when a spirituality that I have spoken anywhere in the world, I owe it to my Master; only the mistakes are mine.

This is the message of Sri Râmakrishna to the modern world. "Do not care for doctrines, do not care for dogmas, or sects, or churches or temples; they count for little compared with the essence of existence in each man which is spirituality, and the more that this is developed in a man, the more powerful is he for good. Earn that first, acquire that, and criticise no one, for all doctrines and creeds have some good in them. Show by your lives that religion does not mean words, nor names, nor sects, but that it means spiritual realization. Only those can understand who have felt. Only those that have attained to spirituality can communicate it to others, can be great teachers of mankind. They alone are the powers of light."

The more such men are produced in a country, the more that country will be raised; and that country where such men absolutely do not exist is simply doomed, nothing can save it. Therefore, my Master's message to mankind is, "Be spiritual and realize truth for yourself." He would have you give up for the sake of your fellow beings. He would have you cease talking about love for your brother, and set to work to prove your words. The time has come for renunciation, for realization, and then you will see the harmony in all the religions of the world. You will know that there is no need of any quarrel, and then only will you be ready to help humanity. To proclaim and make clear the fundamental unity underlying all religions was the mission of my Master. Other teachers have taught special religions which bear their names, but this great Teacher of the nineteenth century made no claim for himself he left every religion undisturbed because he had realized that, in reality, they are all part and parcel of one Eternal Religion.

PARAMHAMSA SRIMAT RAMAKRISHNA

The following brief account of this extraordinary man is taken from an article written by Protap Chunder Mazoomdar, which appeared in the *Theistic Quarterly Review*, October, 1879. It serves to show the sentiments he inspired among his contemporaries. Even the celebrated leader of the Brahmo-Somaj, Keshub Chandra Sen, often came to hear Sri Ramakrishna and was influenced by his teachings to a considerable extent. He was born on the 20th of February, 1833. He left this world on the 16th of August, 1886.

PARAMHAMSA SRIMAT RAMAKRISHNA

MY mind is still floating in the luminous atmosphere which that wonderful man diffuses around him whenever and wherever he goes. My mind is not yet disenchanted of the mysterious and indefinable pathos which he pours into it whenever he meets me. What is there in common between him and me? I, a Europeanized, civilized, self-centered, semi-sceptical, so-called educated reasoner, and he a poor, illiterate, unpolished, half-idolatrous, friendless Hindu devotee? Why should I sit long hours to attend to him, I who have listened to Disraeli and Fawcett, Stanley and Max Müller, and a whole host of European scholars and divines? I who am an ardent disciple and follower of Christ, a friend and admirer of liberal-minded Christian missionaries and preachers, a devoted adherent and worker of the rationalistic Brahmo-Somaj—why should I be spellbound to hear him? And it is not I only, but dozens like me who do the same. He has been interviewed and examined by many, crowds pour in to visit and talk with him. Some of our clever intellectual fools have found nothing in him, some of the contemptuous Christian missionaries would call him an impostor, or a self-deluded enthusiast. I have weighed their objections well, and what I write now I write deliberately.

The Hindu saint is a man under forty. He is a Brahmin by caste, he is well-formed in body naturally, but the dreadful austerities through which his character has developed appear to have disordered his system. Yet, in the midst of this emaciation his face retains a fullness, a child-like tenderness, a profound visible humbleness, an unspeakable sweetness of expression and a smile that I have seen on no other face that I can remember. A Hindu saint is always particular about his externals. He wears the *garua* cloth, eats according to strict forms, refuses to have intercourse with men, and is a rigid observer of caste. He is always proud and professes secret wisdom. He is always *guruji*, a universal counsellor and a dispenser of charms. This man is singularly devoid of such claims. His dress and diet do not differ from those of other men except in the general negligence he shows towards both, and as to caste, he openly breaks it every day. He most vehemently repudiates the title of *guru*, or teacher, he shows impatient displeasure at any exceptional honor which people try to pay to him, and emphatically disclaims the knowledge of secrets and mysteries. He protests against being lionized, and openly shows his strong dislike to be visited and praised by the curious. The society of the worldly-minded and carnally-inclined he carefully shuns. He has nothing extraordinary about him. His religion is his only recommendation. And what is his religion? It is orthodox Hinduism, but Hinduism of a strange type. Râmakrishna Paramhamsa (for that is the name of this saint), is the worshipper of no particular Hindu god. He is not a Shivaite, he is not a Shakta, he is not a Vaishnava, he is not a Vedantist. Yet he is *all these*. He worships Shiva, he worships Kâli, he worships Râma, he worships Krishna, and is a confirmed advocate of Vedantist doctrines. He accepts all the doctrines, all the embodiments, usages, and devotional practices of every religious cult. Each in turn is infallible to him. He is an idolater, yet is a faithful and most devoted meditator of the perfections of the one formless, infinite Deity whom he terms, "*Akhanda Sach-chidânanda,*" ("Indivisible Existence-Knowledge-Bliss.") His religion, unlike the religion of ordinary Hindu *sadhus*, does not mean too much dogma, or controversial proficiency, or the outward worship with flowers and sandal-wood; incense and offering. His religion means ecstasy, his worship means transcendental insight, his whole nature burns day and night with the permanent fire and fever of a strange faith and feeling. His conversation is a ceaseless breaking forth of this inward fire and lasts long hours. While his interlocutors are weary, he, though outwardly feeble, is as fresh as ever. He merges into rapturous ecstasy and outward unconsciousness often during the day, oftenest in conversation when he speaks of his favorite spiritual experiences, or hears any striking response to them. But how is it possible that he has such a fervent regard for all the Hindu deities together? What is the secret of his singular eclecticism? To him each of these deities is a force, an incarnated principle tending to reveal the supreme relation of the soul to that eternal and formless Being Who is unchangeable in His blessedness and the Light of Wisdom.

Take for instance Shiva. The saint views and realizes Shiva as the incarnation of contemplativeness and Yoga. Forgetful of all worldly care and concern, merged and absorbed in *Samâdhi*, in the meditation of the ineffable perfections of the supreme *Brahman*, insensible to pain and privation, toil and loneliness, ever joyful in the blessedness of Divine communion, calm, silent, serene, immovable like the Himâlayas where his abode is, *Mahadeo* is the ideal of all contemplative and self-absorbed men. The venomous serpents of evil and worldliness coil around his beatified form but cannot hurt him. The presence of death surrounds him in various forms of dread and danger, but cannot daunt him. Shiva takes upon himself the burdens and cares of all the world, and swallows the deadliest poison to confer immortality upon others. Shiva renounces all wealth and enjoyment for the benefit of others, makes his faithful wife the companion of his austerities and solitude, and takes the ashes and the tiger skin as his only ornaments. Shiva is the god of the Yogis. And this good man, while expatiating on the attributes of Shiva, would be immersed in the sublimity of his ideal, and become entranced, and remain unconscious for a long time.

Then, perhaps, he would talk of Krishna, whom he realizes as the incarnation of love. "Behold," he says, "the countenance of

Krishna as represented popularly. Does it resemble a man's face, or a woman's? Is there a shadow of sensuality in it; is there a hair of masculine coarseness? It is a tender female face that Krishna has; in it is the fullness of boyish delicacy and girlish grace. By his affectionateness, many sided and multiform, he won the hearts of men and women to the religion of *Bhakti* (Devotion). That Divine love can take the form of every sanctified human relation is the great mission of Krishna to prove. As a loving child monopolizing all the fondness of the hearts of aged parents; as a loving companion and friend attracting the profoundest loyalty and affection of men and brethren; as an admired and adored master, the sweetness and tenderness of whose teaching and whose affectionate persuasions converted girls and women to the self-consecration of a heartfelt piety, Krishna, the beauty and depth of whose character remain still beyond the reach of men's appreciation, introduced the religion of love into Hindustan. Then the good man would say how for long years he dressed himself as a cowherd, or a milkmaid, to be able to realize the experiences of that form of piety in which the human soul was like a faithful wife, and a loyal friend to the loving Spirit who is our Lord and only friend. Krishna is the incarnation of Bhakti. Then in the intensity of that burning love of God which is in his simple heart, the devotee's form and features suddenly grow stiff and motionless, unconsciousness overtakes him, his eyes lose their sight, and tears trickle down his fixed, pale, but smiling face. There is a transcendent sense and meaning in that unconsciousness. What he perceives and enjoys in his soul when he has lost all outward perception who can say? Who will fathom the depth of that insensibility which the love of God produces? But that he sees something, hears, and enjoys when he is dead to all the outward world there is no doubt. If not, why should he, in the midst of that unconsciousness, burst into floods of tears and break out into prayers, songs and utterances the force and pathos of which pierce through the hardest heart, and bring tears to eyes that never before wept under the influence of religion?

Anon he would begin to talk of Kâli, whom he addresses as his mother. She is the incarnation of the *Shakti*, or power of God as displayed in the character and influence of woman. Kâli is the female principle in the nature of the Deity. She tyrannizes over all tyrants. She brings down her husband low upon the ground, and places her foot upon his bosom. She charms and conquers all beings. Yet she is the mother of creation. Her tremendous power is a guarantee that she can save and protect her children, those that come to her as their mother, and ask the shelter of her feet. Her motherly solicitude excites the tenderest filial affection in the hearts of her devotees, and the inspiration of Ramprosad Sen which expressed itself in the most wonderful songs of filial piety ever sung, bears strange testimony to the reality and effectiveness of the worship of Kâli. The adoration of *Shakti* (which literally means Force) is, according to our saint, a child-like, whole-souled, rapturous self-consecration to the motherhood of God as represented by the power and influence of woman. Woman, therefore, has long been renounced by our friend in every material and carnal relation. He has a wife but has never associated with her. Woman, he says, is unconquerable by man except by him who looks up to her as a son. Woman fascinates and keeps the whole world from the love of God. The highest and holiest saints have been brought back to carnality and sin by the nameless power of woman. The absolute conquest of lust has been his lifelong ambition. For long years, therefore, he says, he made the utmost efforts to be delivered from the influence of woman. His heart-rending supplications and prayers for such deliverance, sometimes uttered aloud in his retreat on the river-side, brought crowds of people who bitterly cried when he cried, and could not help blessing him and wishing him success with their whole hearts.

He has successfully escaped the evil of carnality which he dreaded. His Mother to whom he prayed, that is the goddess Kâli, made him recognize every woman as her incarnation, so that he now honors each member of the other sex as his mother. He bows his head to the ground before women, and before little girls; he has insisted upon worshipping not a few of them as a son might worship his mother. The purity of his thoughts and relations towards women is most unique and instructive. It is the opposite of the European idea. It is an attitude essentially, traditionally, gloriously national. Yes, a Hindu *can* honor woman.

"My father," says the Paramhamsa, "was a worshipper of Râma. I, too, have accepted the Râmayat covenant. When I think of the piety of my father, the flowers with which he used to worship his favorite god bloom again in my heart and fill it with Divine fragrance." Râma the truthful and dutiful son, the good and faithful husband, the just and fatherly king, the staunch and affectionate friend, is regarded by him with the love and profound loyalty of a devoted servant. As a master the privilege of whose service is sufficient reward to the favored, faithful servant, as a master in whose dear and matchless service the laying down of life is a delightful duty, as a master who has wholly enslaved the body and soul of his adoring slave, the contemplation of whose holy and glorious worth transcends every thought of remuneration and return, is Râma viewed by Râmakrishna. Hanuman, the renowned follower of Râma, is to him a model of a faithful servitor, a being who was devoted to his master's cause, inspired by such unworldly love and honor, such superhuman faithfulness as scorned alike death and danger, or hope of reward. So the other sin which he spent his life to be free from, is the love of money. The sight of money fills him with strange dread. His avoidance of women and wealth is the whole secret of his matchless moral character. For a long time he practised a singular discipline. He took in one hand a piece of gold and in the other a lump of earth. He would then look at both, repeatedly calling the gold *earth*, and the earth *gold*, and then shuffling the contents of one hand into the other, he would keep up the process until he lost all sense of the difference between the gold and the earth. His ideal of service is absolute unworldliness and freedom from the desire of gain. He loves and serves Râma because Râma is the best and most loving master. The service of the true saint is the service of the purest affection and most unselfish loyalty. Some of the songs he sings expressive of this touching devotedness are exceedingly pathetic, and show how very negligent we often are.

Nor is his reverence confined within Hinduism. For long days he subjected himself to various disciplines to realize the Mahomedan idea of an all-powerful Allah. He let his beard grow, he fed himself on Moslem diet, he continually repeated sentences from the Koran. His reverence for Christ is deep and genuine. He bows his head at the name of Jesus, honors the doctrine of his sonship, and we believe he once or twice attended Christian places of worship. These ideas at all events show the catholic religious culture of this great Hindu saint.

Each form of worship that we have tried to indicate above is to the Paramhamsa a living and most enthusiastic principle of personal religion, and the accounts of discipline and exercise through which he has arrived at his present state of devotional eclectism are most wonderful, although they cannot be published. He never writes anything, seldom argues, he never attempts to instruct, he is continually pouring out his soul in a rhapsody of spiritual utterances, he sings wonderfully, and makes observations of singular wisdom. He unconsciously throws a flood of marvelous light upon the obscurest passages of the Puranic Shastras, and brings out the fundamental principles of the popular Hindu faith with a philosophical clearness which strangely contrasts itself with his simple and illiterate life. These incarnations, he says, are but the forces (*Shakti*) and dispensations (*Lila*) of the eternally wise and blessed *Akhanda Sachchidânanda* who never can be changed or formulated, who is one endless and everlasting ocean of light, truth and joy.

If all his utterances could be recorded they would form a volume of strange and wonderful wisdom. If all his observations on men and things could be reproduced, people might think that the days of prophecy, of primeval, unlearned wisdom had returned. But it is most difficult to render his sayings in English.*

A living evidence of the depth and sweetness of Hindu religion is this good and holy man. He has wholly controlled his flesh. It is full of soul, full of the reality of religion, full of joy, full of blessed purity. As a *Siddha* Hindu ascetic he is a witness of the falsehood and emptiness of the world. His witness appeals to the profoundest heart of every Hindu. He has no other thought, no other occupation, no other relation, no other friend in his humble life than his God. That God is more than sufficient for him. His spotless holiness, his deep unspeakable blessedness, his unstudied, endless wisdom, his childlike peacefulness and affection towards all men, his

* Prof. Max Muller has recently given a number of these sayings to the world in a volume entitled "Ramakrishna, His Life and Sayings."

consuming, all-absorbing love for God are his only reward. And may he long continue to enjoy that reward! Our own ideal of religious life is different, but so long as he is spared to us, gladly shall we sit at his feet to learn from him the sublime precepts of purity, unworldliness, spirituality and inebriation in the love of God.